To my dedicated colleagues
on the Paramus Board
of Education

BRUCE WEBER

SCHOLASTIC BOOK SERVICES
New York Toronto London Auckland Sydney Tokyo

Material for All-Pro Basketball Stars 1980 went to press on September 10, 1979. For each team's opening game roster, see page 88.

The author wishes to thank the public relations directors of the NBA teams and the league's media department, who facilitated the production of this book.

Cover photo: Focus on Sports

ISBN 0-590-31238-3

12 11 10 9 8 7 6 5 4 3 2 1   1   0 1 2 3 4 5/8

CONTENTS

Lloyd "All-World" Free might
not have been All-World last
year, but his 28.8 scoring made
him an All-Pro.

1979
ALL-PRO
TEAM

Forward:	Bobby Dandridge
Forward:	Walter Davis
Forward:	Elvin Hayes
Forward:	Marques Johnson
Center	Kareem Abdul-Jabbar
Center	Moses Malone
Guard:	Lloyd Free
Guard:	George Gervin
Guard:	David Thompson
Guard:	Paul Westphal

Forward
BOBBY DANDRIDGE
Washington Bullets

In a league loaded with super-small forwards, there are few better than Bob Dandridge. Dr. J wasn't good enough to make the All-Pro team in 1979. But Dandridge, the guy who makes the Washington Bullets fly, did.

Bobby is a worker, a hard worker. There's no flash, no pizzazz in his game. His teammate, Elvin Hayes, is colorful. If the players' clothes matched their games, Elvin would be a snappy tuxedo. Dandridge would be a pair of jeans and a blue work shirt.

Bob, who's 6-6 and 195 pounds, has played on two NBA championship teams. Neither time was he the star. The first time (1971), it was Milwaukee with Kareem Abdul-Jabbar. The second time (1978), it was Washington with Hayes and Wes Unseld.

That doesn't bother Dandridge. He doesn't want to be famous. He wants to be rich. Last year he missed pre-season training, waiting to work out a better money deal with the Bullets. Money has always been a big thing for Bob, going back to his rookie season in Milwaukee, nine years ago.

None of this is designed to make Bob the most popular Bullet among the owners, players, or fans. But they respect Dandridge for the job he does so well. Scoring? Sure. Dandridge averaged 20.4 ppg last last season. He also dished off 365 assists and plucked down 447 rebounds.

Defense? That too. Dandridge was a first-team choice on the NBA Defensive Team.

One more thing. When the chips are down, the Bullets are likely to go to Dandridge. He does it all.

Forward
WALTER DAVIS
Phoenix Suns

When NBA scouts look for players who own all the basic skills, they usually check the Univeristy of Dean Smith. Never heard of it? How about the University of North Carolina? That's where Smith has been turning out sound basketball players for nearly 20 years.

Chances are that Dean has never coached anyone sounder than the Suns' Walt Davis. His All-Pro teammate, Paul Westphal, watches Davis with awe. "There is no quicker forward," says Westphal, "and no one anywhere can shoot jump shots with him. But best of all, he'll do anything to help us win."

The 6-6, 198-pounder, who turned 25 years old just before this season, is the master of that little 8- to 10-foot jumper. That's basketball's make or break shot. The fans expect you to make it. But if you don't, you're a bum. Walter Davis always makes it!

A star of the 1976 U.S. Olympic champions (coached by Dean Smith), Davis is simply one of the smoothest players in the business. "No one can go from a standing start to full speed faster than Davis," says Phoenix coach John MacLeod. "That actually makes it tough for him. It never looks like he's going all out. He makes the game look too easy."

Walt was never better than in '79. His 56.1% shooting average was the best ever by a Sun and the best ever by an NBA forward with a 20-point-or-better average. Walt's average: 23.6 ppg, good for 10th in the league. He also set personal bests for field goals, assists, steals, and single-game scoring (42 versus Portland).

Is Davis consistent? You bet. His seven-point outing against Seattle last January marked the *only* time in his career that he failed to make double figures!

ELVIN HAYES
Washington Bullets

There are all sorts of new faces on the 1979 All-Pro team — and one very solid old face. The graybeard is Elvin Hayes.

And whether he's 34 (as the record books say) or 32 (as Elvin himself insists), he still seems to have lots of good basketball left.

The 6-9½, 235-pounder from the University of Houston is one of the best all-around players ever. "He can do it all," says his coach, Dick Motta, who should know. "When I was coaching Chicago, I never knew how good Big E. was. Now, after coaching him for two seasons, I can really appreciate him."

As usual, Elvin played in all 82 regular-season games for Washington in '79. (In fact, in 11 seasons Elvin has missed only five games.) He was as good as ever, averaging 21.8 points per game, 12.1 rebounds (sixth best in the league), and 2.32 blocked shots. Not bad for an old man.

"As hard as he works," says Motta, "it's amazing that he's still around. No one works as hard as Elvin. No big man ever moved up and down the court as much as he does. I try to give him a little extra rest every night. But every time I sit him down he pesters me: 'When can I go back in?' Elvin comes to play — all night, every night."

Hayes wasn't always the Big E. Fact is, until his senior year of high school he was the Little E. He was only 5-10. That's when he started growing, which created problems for a poor kid in Rayville, Louisiana. No money meant no clothes and no shoes that fit. It was tough.

That isn't a problem anymore. Elvin earns $450,000 a year from the Bullets. To hear coach Dick Motta tell the story, he's worth every penny.

MARQUES JOHNSON
Milwaukee Bucks

The Bucks didn't make the playoffs last season. That was a disappointment. But you can pin the blame anywhere but on Marques Johnson's shoulders.

The ex-UCLA great might just be the NBA's top forward after only his second season. Why not? He does it all for Milwaukee. The 6-7, 218-pounder averaged 25.6 points per game in '79, third best in the league and best among all front-court players. He also led Milwaukee in 12 of 21 offensive departments, including rebounding (586, 7.6 per game) and shooting (55%).

Marques is one of the most exciting players in the game. Last season, the Bucks worked on the "Alley Oop" stuff play that made David Thompson famous. The work paid off. In 39 home games, Johnson had 96 dunks, most of them of the slam-dunk variety. But it isn't just the Milwaukee fans who love Johnson. In the All-Star game voting, he drew more votes than any other Western Conference player.

Johnson is just about the perfect-looking basketball player. His shoulders are enormous, like a football tackle's. Then the body tapers to a thin, athlete's waist. The legs are all-powerful. They make Johnson one of the NBA's best leapers.

Best of all, Marques enjoys playing basketball. "Everyone knows how great he is in the games," said his coach, Don Nelson, last season. "Well, he's just as good, he works just as hard, in practices, too. That tells you something about Marques."

Center
KAREEM
ABDUL-JABBAR
Los Angeles Lakers

Let's face it. Laker fans are spoiled. For the last four years, they've been blessed with the finest center in the pro game, perhaps the best ever. Their man, Kareem Abdul-Jabbar, is 32 now. He may be getting just a little long in the tooth. He may have lost a pinch off the top of his game. Still, just about every team in the league — except, perhaps, Houston and San Diego — would part with half the franchise for the Lakers' big guy.

But the L.A. fans aren't happy. They aren't happy with the whole team. So whom do they take it out on? Their star, of course. "Sure they pick on me," says Kareem. "Why not? I'm a natural target. I'm too big to miss."

Is Kareem happy about the abuse? Of course not. He really doesn't deserve it. He had another outstanding, All-Pro season in '79, his ninth in 10 years. The numbers were about as good as ever. The 7-2 (or is it 7-4?) ex-UCLA great played in all 82 games, put in 39½ minutes per outing, hit 57.7% of his shots (second best in the league), scored 23.8 ppg (eighth best), pulled down 1,025 rebounds (third best), dished off 431 assists, and blocked 316 shots (3.95 per game, best in the NBA for the third time). Laker fan or not, you can't sneer at those figures.

Off a not-bad 47-35 season (and a playoff victory over Denver), the Lakers brought in a bunch of new faces. But the old face, the one perched above the league's tallest neck, still belongs to the team's main man. Don't cry, Laker fans. The rest of the NBA is still jealous!

MOSES MALONE

Houston Rockets

If Moses Malone had gone to college, chances are he'd have been the NBA's Rookie of the Year last year. He didn't, of course. Instead of enrolling at the University of Maryland, the Petersburg (Virginia) high school product turned pro with the Utah Stars of the ABA. Now, after five pro seasons, Moses owns one Most Valuable Player trophy and a new three-year contract at around a million bucks a year.

Maryland coach Lefty Driesell still moans about the day Big Mo got away. And early in Moses' pro career, it looked like the high school-to-pro jump might have been a mistake.

It's clear now, however, that there was no mistake. The 6-10, 220-pounder might just be the finest offensive rebounder ever to pull on a pair of shorts. Last season, he pulled down 587 missed Houston shots. That was an NBA record. He wasn't bad on the defensive boards, either. His total of 1,444 'bounds gave him a 17.6 rebounds-per-game average, an incredible 4.8 better than runner-up Rich Kelley of the Jazz!

Of course, Moses does more than rebound. Last season he played 3,390 minutes, more than any other NBA player, and tossed in 24.8 points per game, fifth best in the league. The Rockets weren't that talented. But with the big man doing everything asked of him, they finished 47-35, only one game behind Central Division leader San Antonio.

Malone's best night? Perhaps it was last February 9 when he picked off 37 rebounds, 19 of the offensive variety. The MVP Award was never in doubt.

LLOYD FREE
San Diego Clippers

For his first three years as a pro, Lloyd Free tried to live up to his nickname, "All-World." It wasn't easy. His team, the Philadelphia 76ers, was loaded. Lloyd did a lot of talking, almost none of it on the court.

Last season, Philly set Free free. It was the best thing that ever happened to the 6-3 guard from Brooklyn, New York. In San Diego, with the brand-new Clippers (formerly the Buffalo Braves), Lloyd took his act onto the court. He was just about as good as he always said he was.

Given a chance, Lloyd put in 38 minutes a game, hit 48.1% of his shots (many from as far away as downtown San Diego), and poured in 28.8 points per game, second only to San Antonio's machine, George Gervin.

"World," as his friends call him, still didn't set any worlds on fire on defense. But he showed that he knew how to hit an open man. His 340 assists were second on the Clipper club to speedy Randy Smith.

Free's biggest booster in San Diego is coach Gene Shue. Shue, who coached Free in Philadelphia, leaped at the chance to pick Lloyd up when the Sixers let him go. "He's my man," said Shue. On the way to a 43-39 season record (the 1978 Braves were 27-55), Shue said, "I don't know where we'd be without Lloyd. He does so many things so well. He can beat you so many ways."

Can Free ever really earn his nickname, "All-World"? His new fans in San Diego think so.

GEORGE GERVIN
San Antonio Spurs

Too bad George Gervin doesn't play in
New York or Chicago or Los Angeles.

Then, maybe everyone would know him. As it is, the real fans know that George is simply one of the hottest offensive machines ever. But, since he makes his living in San Antonio, the NBA's smallest city, some folks still don't know who he is.

Gervin's 29.6 ppg scoring last season won him his second straight NBA scoring title. Five other players have done it — super-names like George Mikan, Neil Johnston, Wilt Chamberlain, Kareem Abdul-Jabbar, and Bob McAdoo. All of them were front-court players. Gervin is the only guard in history to win back-to-back titles.

The 6-8 San Antonio "Iceman" does everything coach Doug Moe asks of him. Check these numbers. His 91 blocks were unmatched by all but one in the league. He led the Spurs and the NBA's backcourt men in shooting percentage with 54.1%.

Stopping Gervin is an almost impossible task for Spurs' opponents. Sometimes he shoots with his left hand, other times with his right, and occasionally with both hands. He drives left or right or down the middle. He's just as deadly under the basket as he is 25 feet away.

How did Gervin get his nickname, "The Iceman"? Simple. He's just the coolest, calmest customer around. When the Spurs are in trouble, there's one guy they always turn to — "The Iceman."

There will be lots of new numbers on the San Antonio roster this season. But the fans' favorite number will still be on hand: it's 44, and it belongs to George Gervin.

DAVID THOMPSON

Denver Nuggets

The Denver Nuggets struggled in 1979. The team lost its division title to the Kansas City Kings. It lost early in the NBA playoffs. And it lost coach Larry Brown to UCLA.

But one thing didn't change in Denver. It was — and is — David Thompson. In

Colorado, they call the 6-4 Thompson "The Skywalker." That's the same name as the *Star Wars* hero. But Luke Skywalker had to use rocket power to soar through the air. "Skywalker" Thompson uses leg power. Fact is, he's more like Superman. You know, he leaps tall buildings in a single bound. And the names of those "buildings" include Abdul-Jabbar, Gilmore, Malone, etc.

Last year wasn't Thompson's best. In the first two months of the season, he suffered from a pulled groin, a virus infection, a shoulder injury, a bruised knee, and a slight concussion. All season long, whenever D. T. hit high gear, something bad happened. Still, he had a fine year, with a 24.0 ppg scoring average, a 51.2% shooting mark, 225 assists, and 82 blocked shots. Among the Nuggets, only 6-11 Kim Hughes (102) had more.

Every defender in the league has a David Thompson story. "We had him trapped," says one. "The passing lanes were blocked. So he stepped through and jammed the ball home." The rest of the tales sound almost the same.

Do the fans appreciate "The Skywalker"? You bet. In the voting for the NBA All-Star Game last year, no Western Conference player earned more ballots than Thompson. His outstanding All-Star performance showed the fans they knew something. When David won the MVP trophy, he became only the second player (Julius Erving is the other) to win the award in both the ABA and NBA All-Star Games.

Guard
PAUL WESTPHAL
Phoenix Suns

Paul Westphal has it made. The veteran guard from Phoenix was happy to make the 1979 All-Pro team, but not really surprised. "I don't start out aiming to become an All-Leaguer," he says. "But it's nice to know that people recognize your performance."

It's hard to miss Westphal's All-Star performances. For the fourth straight year, the 6-4, 185-pound ex-USC star led the Suns in scoring. His 24.0 ppg average was tied with Denver's David Thompson for sixth best in the league. Paul also had his best year ever in assists (529, 6.5 per game), shooting (53.5%), foul shooting (83.7%), and one-game assists (14, three different times).

"It's hard for opposing defenses to prepare for Westy," says Phoenix coach John MacLeod. "There's just no scouting report on him. He can shoot from anywhere, he can hit with either hand, he can direct a fast break, or he can be the pass receiver. He can hit just about as often from 18 feet as 10."

Paul doesn't have all the physical gifts of some other All-Pros. If the league's guards ever held a sprint race to determine something important, Westy would be in trouble. Speed isn't one of his strengths. But quickness is. And few guards move without the ball as well as Westphal.

One of these years, Phoenix is going to go all the way in the NBA playoffs. And when they do, Arizona's favorite Sun is going to be California-born Paul Westphal.

Kansas City drove a Ford—
Rookie-of-the-Year
Phil Ford—
to the Midwest Division title in '79.

1979
ALL-ROOKIE
TEAM

Forward:	Terry Tyler
Center:	Mychal Thompson
Guard:	Ron Brewer
Guard:	Phil Ford
Guard/Forward:	Reggie Theus

Forward
TERRY TYLER
Detroit Pistons

Terry Tyler can't remember a time when Dick Vitale wasn't his coach. For three years at the University of Detroit, the 6-7 Tyler and the much, much shorter Vitale made a winning pair. Then, after Vitale and the Pistons made Tyler a low second-round draft choice, Tyler proved to the pros that his college coach made him quite a player.

In his first NBA season, Tyler averaged 12.9 ppg, plucked down 7.9 rebounds per game, and blocked 2.45 shots per outing, fifth best in the league and ahead of such noted rejectors as Elvin Hayes, Artis Gilmore, and a host of others.

So Terry, proud of his rookie season, spent the off-season resting on his laurels. Wrong! Tyler and many of his teammates packed their bags and headed west, to the Los Angeles Summer Pro League. It was hard work for what should have been a fun off-season. But Tyler thinks it paid off.

"I had a chance to work on my weaknesses," he says. "Last year, for instance, I hit only 66% of my free throws. During the summer it was 80%. I hope I've solved my problems there."

Terry also had a chance to try different positions. "That's one secret to staying in the NBA," he says. "You have to be able to play more than one position. I want to be able to go from defensing a big forward to a little forward, even at mid-game."

Although he jumps well enough to play the bigger guys, Terry prefers guarding the quick forwards. Either way, the Pistons (and Dick Vitale) have a winner!

Center
MYCHAL
THOMPSON
Portland Trail Blazers

The greatest player ever to come out of
the Bahamas! As pro basketball players

go, that's not saying much. But for Mike Thompson, the super-rookie of the Portland Trail Blazers, it's something he's really proud of.

Thompson, the Blazers' (and the league's) top draft pick in 1978, has gone from the Islands to the University of Minnesota to Portland. And he has been great everywhere.

When Portland opened up shop last season, both Bill Walton and Maurice Lucas were sidelined. Walton, of course, missed the entire season before moving to San Diego. Lucas missed the first 10 games. What kept Portland on the road to the Western playoffs was their rookie star, Thompson.

The 6-10, 225-pounder tossed in 14.7 points per game, hit a solid 49% from the field, was third on the club (behind Tom Owens and the later-healthy Lucas) in rebounding with 604, and led Portland in blocked shots with 134.

For a big guy, Mike is beautifully coordinated. And he's very quick. Like most rookies, he had early problems on defense last year. But, by season's end, he was holding his own with the Dr. J's and Walt Davis's who can really mess up a defensive forward's life.

The proof of Thompson's late-season arrival is found in the stats. Over the last 17 games, Mike averaged 20.9 ppg and hit 54.3% of his shots.

Though a broken leg threatened to keep Thompson out of the Blazers' lineup deep into the 1980 season, the Bahamas' main man may soon become Portland's too.

RON BREWER
Portland Trail Blazers

As the 1979 Blazers suffered through the

worst of times, they also looked forward to better. One key to Portland's improved fortunes has to be guard Ron Brewer, the 6-4 fireball from Arkansas.

Early last season, Brewer was doing all those things that make coaches scream, "Rookies! Ugh!" For instance, Ron would forget a coverage, give up an easy bucket, then let it get him down the rest of the night.

By the middle of the season, when the injury-riddled Blazers really needed him, Ron had turned it around. Brewer learned from his early mistakes — and that's the sign of tomorrow's top pros.

"Ron wasn't aggressive enough," says coach Jack Ramsay. "He wasn't taking the ball to the basket. And he seemed to be forgetting that he could jump over buildings. Once he got over that, he was on his way."

That meant a 13.3 ppg average on 49.4% shooting. No Blazer rookie guard ever did better. As proof positive of Brewer's late-season improvement, he averaged 15.2 ppg over the final 44 contests. Can the man jump? Check this: Brewer blocked 79 opponents' shots. Only 6-10 Mychal Thompson (134) and 6-9 Maurice Lucas (81) had more.

One night last February, Brewer popped in 11 of his first 15 shots and went on to ring up his season's high of 30 points. No one was more impressed than Houston's Robert Reid. He had the job of stopping Brewer. "Brewer has lots of talent," says Reid. "Even better, he really knows how to play this game."

Guard
PHIL FORD
Kansas City Kings

Want to join the Phil Ford fan club? You'll have to line up — right behind Cotton Fitzsimmons and Otis Birdsong. Coach Fitzsimmons took over a 31-51, last-place Kings team. With Ford's help, the club went 48-34 last season, won the Midwest Division title, and made Cotton the NBA's Coach of the Year.

Birdsong, good as a rookie, was great as a sophomore, playing next to Ford in the Kaycee backcourt. Did he enjoy it? Listen: "Playing with Phil Ford," said Birdsong, "is like having Christmas every day!"

The jump from College Player of the Year was a piece of cake for the 6-2, 170-pounder from North Carolina. The man Cotton Fitzsimmons calls "the best point guard ever" had eight or more assists 41 times, 20 or more points 29 times, finished fourth in assists (8.6 per game), and wound up fifth in steals (2.2). He did everything except make rookie mistakes.

The Kansas City-Phil Ford marriage wasn't exactly made in heaven. In fact, it almost didn't come off. Phil and his college coach, Dean Smith, begged the Kings not to draft Phil. "I wanted to be with a winner," said Ford.

For a while, Phil said he would return to North Carolina (as a Smith assistant) or move to Italy (to play). Finally, Phil gave in. He signed with the Kings. The rest is history. Phil wanted to be with a winner. He was. He made Kaycee a winner.

Do you think the Kings were only a flash in the pan? Ford has a better idea!

Guard-Forward
REGGIE THEUS
Chicago Bulls

Chicago fans didn't have much to cheer about last year. But at least they had Reggie Theus. The smooth, powerful floor-leader from the University of Nevada-Las Vegas excited the fans every night, no matter how badly things were going for the home team.

It came as somewhat of a surprise. Except for the hardship rule, the 6-7, 205-pound Theus would have been at Las Vegas last season. And he would still have been at forward, instead of at the guard spot he proved so good at.

Reggie averaged 16.3 ppg last season, best among NBA rookies. "He's the best rookie scoring guard I've ever seen," said one opponent. And why not? Reggie set new Bulls' rookie records for shots taken and made, minutes played, points per game, free throws attempted and made, field-goal percentage, assists, and steals. Not a bad year's work!

There's no telling how good Theus could have been if he hadn't been forced to be a play-making guard last season. If he ever gets a chance to play off the ball, he could be impossible. Thanks to his size, he's also one of the finest young defensive guards in the league.

New coach Jerry Sloan says, "You have to like Reggie. He's quiet, but that doesn't stop him from being a leader. He's confident of his ability and it shows. No matter whom he's on the floor with, youngster or vet, he's in charge. Reggie is always in control."

Billy "The Whopper" Paultz helped San Antonio to the Central title in '79. Can he do it again?

A LOOK BACK —
A LOOK AHEAD

(Team statistical leaders must
meet NBA minimum qualification
standards.)

SEATTLE SUPERSONICS

Jack Sikma

Dennis Johnson

Hail to the champions — because, next year, who knows. No NBA champion has repeated since the 1968 and 1969 Boston Celtics. There must be a lesson there somewhere, students of history.

History aside, the Sonics and coach Len Wilkens are confident they can do it again. Barring a court order that would send 6-8 Lonnie Shelton (13.5 and 51.9% shooting) and/or 6-2 rookie Vinnie Johnson to the Knicks, Seattle seems set at every position.

The 6-4 DJ — no, not a disc jockey but playoff MVP Dennis Johnson — can do it all. He's super-strong inside (leading to a 15.9 ppg average), and is the best shot-blocking guard in the NBA (97 rejects a year ago). If he's happy (he wasn't during the summer — money problems), he'll team perfectly with 6-2 Gus Williams. The ex-Southern Cal star was the Sonics' No. 2 scorer (19.2) and ball-hawker (158 steals).

The champs are solid up front, too. 6-11 blond-bomber Jack Sikma (15.6 ppg, 12.4 rebounds) can — and has — played brilliantly at forward and center. If center Tom LaGarde (out most of last season) is healthy, Sikma may return to forward — thus moving Shelton to the bench. Either way, 6-7 John "JJ" Johnson (11.0) should be set at quick forward.

"Downtown" Freddie Brown, the team's 6-3 captain, may be the best sixth man in the NBA. The 14.0 ppg scorer is like a second coach on the floor.

Do the rich get richer? Seattle does. The draft brought 6-9 James Bailey of Rutgers and another Johnson, 6-2 Vinnie from Baylor.

Another championship? It's possible.

TEAM LEADERS — 1979

Minutes Played: Sikma, 2,958	Assists: J. Johnson, 358
Field-Goal Percentage: Shelton, .519	Steals: Williams, 158
Free-Throw Percentage: Brown, .888	Blocks: D. Johnson, 97
Rebounds: Sikma, 1,013	Scoring: Williams, 19.2

DRAFT CHOICES

1.	James Bailey	6-9	Rutgers
1a.	Vinnie Johnson	6-1	Baylor
2.	John Moore	6-1½	Texas
3.	Choice to Cleveland		
4.	James Donaldson	7-2	Washington State
4a.	Richie Allen	6-7	Cal. State-Dominguez
5.	PASS		
6.	PASS		
7.	PASS		
8.	PASS		
9.	PASS		
10.	PASS		

PHOENIX SUNS

Truck Robinson

Alvan Adams

Coach John MacLeod and general manager Jerry Colangelo kept most of the same cast together in Phoenix — and why not? The Suns went 50-32 last year (two games behind NBA champ Seattle), then came within an eyelash of unseating the Sonics in the playoff semi-finals.

There's super-strength in the backcourt with 6-4 All-Pro Paul Westphal (24.0, 529 assists). There's All-Pro small forward 6-6 Walt Davis (23.6, 373 rebounds), one of the smartest players in the game. And there's mid-season pick-up 6-7 Truck Robinson at power forward (21.1, 802 boards).

Sun fans aren't thrilled with 6-9 (but only 212 pounds) Alvan Adams at center. They think Phoenix won't win without a Jabbar-Walton-Gilmore-type giant. But Adams (17.8, 705 rebounds) is, perhaps, the best passing center in the league (360 assists in '79).

The Suns have plenty of depth with forwards 6-6 Gar Heard (6.3) and late-season surprise 6-7 Joel Kramer (5.9 and 54.2% playoff shooting). Top backcourt reserve 6-2 Mike Bratz (8.1, but 10.6 in the playoffs) could start for almost any team except one which features Westphal and 6-4 Don Buse (7.8, 156 assists).

The draft provided little help, but Phoenix didn't need much. One note of caution: The Pacific Division may be the NBA's most improved.

TEAM LEADERS — 1979

Minutes Played: Westphal, 2,641
Field-Goal Percentage: Davis, .561
Free-Throw Percentage: Westphal, .837
Rebounds: Adams, 705*

Assists: Westphal, 529
Steals: Buse, 156
Blocks: Adams, 63*
Scoring: Westphal, 24.0

*Truck Robinson had 802 rebounds for the season (225 in 26 games with Phoenix) and 75 blocked shots (12 with Phoenix).

DRAFT CHOICES

1.	Kyle Macy	6-3	Kentucky
2.	Johnny High	6-3	Nevada-Reno
3.	Al Green	6-2	LSU
4.	Malcolm Cesare	6-9	Florida
5.	Mark Eaton	7-4	Cyprus Junior College
6.	Dale Shackelford	6-6	Syracuse
7.	Ollie Matson	6-6	Pepperdine
8.	Charley Jones	6-9	Albany (GA) State
9.	Hosea Champine	6-4	Robert Morris (PA)
10.	Korky Nelson	6-11	Santa Clara

LOS ANGELES LAKERS

Spencer Haywood

Norm Nixon

What's new in Los Angeles? Practically everything. Owner Jerry Buss has replaced Jack Kent Cooke. Utah Jazz forward Spencer Haywood has traded places with Laker Adrian Dantley. But the top new face belongs to the NBA's top draft pick, 6-8 Earvin Johnson of Michigan State.

L.A. fans hope that "Magic" Johnson can cast a spell on the Lakers as he did for the Spartan national college champs last year. Probably the biggest passing guard in basketball history, Johnson should blend well with last year's starters, 6-2 Ron Boone (7.4) and flicker-quick 6-2 Norm Nixon (17.1, 201 steals), to give the Lakers one of the best backcourts in the pros.

Center is no problem for Los Angeles. 7-2 Kareem Abdul-Jabbar, now 32 years old, is still capable of playing as well as ever. The team leader in just about every important offensive and defensive department, Kareem should blend well with Johnson.

With the guards and center solid, the Lakers have one probelm — forward. New addition Haywood, an eight-year vet who averaged 20.9 ppg with the Knicks and Jazz last year, might help. But he has problems on the defensive end and often needs a ball of his own. At 6-6 and 190, Jamaal Wilkes (18.6) may lack the strength to play some of the tougher forwards in the NBA. 6-8 Kenny Carr (7.4) and 6-9 Don Ford (6.7) have disappointed so far.

New coach Jack McKinney has the raw materials with which to build a championship team. But playing in the league's toughest division, it won't be easy.

TEAM LEADERS — 1979

Minutes Played: Abdul-Jabbar, 3,157
Field-Goal Percentage:
    Abdul-Jabbar, .577
Free-Throw Percentage: Dantley, .854
Rebounds: Abdul-Jabbar, 1,025

Assists: Abdul-Jabbar, 431
Steals: Nixon, 201
Blocks: Abdul-Jabbar, 316
Scoring: Abdul-Jabbar, 23.8

DRAFT CHOICES

1.	"Magic" Johnson	6-8	Michigan State
1a.	Brad Holland	6-3	UCLA
2.	Oliver Mack	6-3	East Carolina
2a.	Victor King	6-9	Louisiana Tech
2b.	Mark Young	6-10	Fairfield
3.	Walter Daniels	6-2	Georgia
4.	Ray White	6-5	Mississippi State
4a.	Ricky Reed	6-0	Temple
5.	PASS		
6.	PASS		
7.	PASS		
8.	PASS		
9.	PASS		
10.	PASS		

PORTLAND TRAIL BLAZERS

Tom Owens

Maurice Lucas

Shed no tears for the Portland Trail Blazers. Sure they lost their "Franchise," Bill Walton, to San Diego. But they played all year last year (45 wins, 37 losses) without the redhead, and his departure brings tough 6-8 Kermit Washington and a bunch of cash and draft choices.

Coach Jack Ramsay, building for the past two years in the belief that Walton might not be back, has his club poised for a run at the Pacific title.

Talk about young talent. Portland had three outstanding rookies in '79, including 6-10 Mychal Thompson (14.7), the Blazers' top shot-blocker, 6-4 Ron Brewer (13.3), and improving 6-19 Clemon Johnson (3.2).

Late-blooming 6-10 Tom Owens finally arrived in his seventh pro year, leading Portland in minutes played, shooting, and rebounding, while finishing second on the club in scoring (18.5). The big forward, of course, is powerhouse 6-9 Maurice Lucas (20.4). After the Walton settlement, the rumormill had Lucas moving elsewhere. But wherever he plays, the man is tough. (Mike Thompson's mid-summer broken leg, which promised to keep the big guy sidelined until mid-season, was a factor in Ramsay's thinking.)

The backcourt, with 6-3 Lionel Hollins (15.3), 6-1 T.R. Dunn (7.7), 6-5 Larry Steele (7.2), and 6-1 Dave Twardzik (10.4) is solid, and top draftee Jim Paxson of Dayton makes it even better.

Jack Ramsay, master builder, is set for years to come.

TEAM LEADERS — 1979

Minutes Played: Owens, 2,791
Field-Goal Percentage: Owens, .548
Free-Throw Percentage: Twardzik, .873
Rebounds: Owens, 740

Assists: Hollins, 325
Steals: Hollins, 114
Blocks: Thompson, 134
Scoring: Lucas, 20.4

DRAFT CHOICES

1.	Jim Paxson	6-5	Dayton
2.	Andrew Fields	6-8	Cheyney State (PA)
3.	Mickey Fox	6-0	St. Mary's (Canada)
4.	Daryll Robinson	6-4	Appalachian State
5.	Matt White	6-10	Pennsylvania
6.	Ray Ellis	7-0	Pepperdine
7.	Jeff Tropf	6-7	Central Michigan
8.	Willie Pounds	6-7	Chaminade (HI)
9.	Stan Eckwood	6-3	Harding (AR)
10.	Kelvin Small	6-7	Oregon

Pacific Division
SAN DIEGO CLIPPERS

Bill Walton

Nick Weatherspoon

Color San Diego red. Not for embarrassment but for hair. Red hair — like the hair on Bill Walton's head and chin. Bill will make or break the San Diego franchise.

The 6-11, 225-pounder from UCLA and the Portland Trail Blazers hasn't been healthy in a season and a half. But when he was, he was the dominant force in pro basketball. A solid Walton is the kind of player championships grow around. Still, Walton has never played a full season, missing over 200 games during four years before the completely lost 1978-79 campaign. The Clippers risked $6,000,000 to sign the smooth, powerful Walton, then gave up tough Kermit Washington, a pile of draft choices, and a ton of cash to satisfy Portland and NBA commissioner Larry O'Brien. Was Bill worth the risk and the price? Stay tuned.

Elsewhere, the surprising (43-39 last year) Clippers are reasonably solid. 6-2 Lloyd "All World" Free (28.8) was the NBA's No. 2 scorer a year ago. With more strength up front, the confident Free will get better. He'll miss his backcourt partner, speedy 6-3 Randy Smith (20.5), who was moved to Cleveland right after the Walton compensation ruling.

A couple of retreads helped San Diego a year ago and should help again. 6-7 Nick Weatherspoon (13.8) came off the Chicago Bulls' scrap heap to become a San Diego starter. Ex-UCLA great 6-9 Sidney Wicks (9.8) has been making the most of what could be his last chance as a pro.

Last year's top rookie, 6-4 Freeman Williams (10.4), should improve. But this year's draft looked poor on paper.

TEAM LEADERS — 1979

Minutes Played: Smith, 3,111
Field-Goal Percentage: Nater, .569
Free-Throw Percentage: Smith, .813
Rebounds: Washington, 800

Assists: Smith, 395
Steals: Smith, 177
Blocks: Washington, 121
Scoring: Free, 28.8

DRAFT CHOICES

1.	Choice to New Jersey		
2.	Choice to Chicago		
3.	Tom Channel	6-3	Boston University
4.	Lionel Garrett	6-9	Southern
5.	Greg Joyner	6-7	Middle Tennessee
6.	Bob Bender	6-2	Duke
7.	Jene Grey	6-4	LeMoyne
8.	Renaldo Lawrence	6-4	Appalachian State
9.	Mike Dodd	6-5	San Diego State
10.	Greg Hunter	6-6	Loyola Marymount

GOLDEN STATE WARRIORS

John Lucas

Robert Parish

The Warriors don't have much luck. They just happen to play in the toughest division in the NBA. And they happen not to have enough talent to pull it off.

Anytime your team revolves around its guards, you have problems. In 6-4 Phil Smith and 6-3 John Lucas, the Warriors have two of the best. Smith (19.9) had played in 305 straight games when he went down with a torn achilles tendon last February. Lucas, the NBA's best tennis player (he's a pro), averaged 16.1 points and 9.3 assists per game, the latter figure second best in the league.

Big (7-0) Robert Parish came into his own as a fourth-year man last season. He tied Elvin Hayes for sixth place in the NBA rebounding derby, was fourth in blocked shots (2.86), and became the Golden State scoring leader (17.2) with Smith out of action.

The weak spot? It's at forward. 6-7 Sonny Parker (15.2) came fast last season. 6-7 Tom Abernethy (6.0) started on the opposite side late last year. He'll get help from 6-7 Purvis Short (10.6), who started 65 games in '79.

On the hopeful list there's ex-Celtic superstar 6-3 Jo Jo White, who averaged 12.3 ppg in 29 Warrior games, and second-year man 6-3 Ray Townsend (4.7), who may still make it as a pro.

The draft, minus a first-round choice, produced 6-7 Danny Salisbury of Pan American and 6-5 Cheese Johnson of Wichita State, either of whom might help.

TEAM LEADERS — 1979

Minutes Played: Lucas, 3,095
Field-Goal Percentage: Parker, .502
Free-Throw Percentage: White, .880
Rebounds: Parish, 916

Assists: Lucas, 762
Steals: Lucas, 152
Blocks: Parish, 217
Scoring: Parish, 17.2*

*Phil Smith averaged 19.9 ppg, but played in only 59 games and scored only 1,172 points. NBA requires 70 games or 1,400 points to qualify.

DRAFT CHOICES

1.	Choice to New York		
2.	Danny Salisbury	6-7	Pan American
3.	Lynbert Johnson	6-5	Wichita State
4.	Ron Ripley	6-10	Green Bay (WI)
4a.	Jerry Sichting	6-1	Purdue
5.	George Lett	6-7	Centenary
6.	Jim Mitchem	6-9	DePaul
7.	Ren Watson	6-9	Virginia Commonwealth
8.	Mario Butler	6-9	Briarcliff
9.	Gene Ransom	6-0	California
10.	Kevin Heenan	6-4	Cal. State Fullerton

KANSAS CITY KINGS

Otis Birdsong

Scott Wedman

From the basement to the penthouse in only one season. That was the story of the Kansas City Kings in '79. The outlook for '80? A playoff team, for sure. But first place? Maybe not.

Rookie-of-the-Year Phil Ford (15.9), the 6-2 ex-North Carolina star, brought all the pieces together for Kaycee. His 8.6 assist average (fourth best in the NBA) helped turn backcourt mate 6-4 Otis Birdsong (21.7) into one of the best guards in the league.

The Kings' front line looks like it belongs in the uniforms of the Kansas City Chiefs. Burly is the word for 6-7, 235-pound Bill Robinzine (13.4), Kaycee's team leader in shooting and the second-best rebounder (638). Not-so-small forward 6-7, 219-pound Scott Wedman (18.3) began showing his 1976 All-Rookie team form last season.

And 6-10, 233-pounder Sam Lacey (10.6) starts the new year with a long-term contract.

That group — all first-round Kaycee draft choices over the years — helped make coach Cotton Fitzsimmons the NBA's 1979 Coach of the Year. To repeat, Cotton will have to find better bench strength. Some of it may come from top draftee 6-6 Reggie King of Alabama and third-rounder 6-4 Terry Crosby. A healthy 7-3 Tom Burleson (7.8) — he missed 26 games last year — will also help.

The roof on the Kings' Kemper Arena blew in after last season. That means Kaycee will play all or most of its 1980 games in the old Municipal Arena. If the Kings play well, maybe their fans will blow the roof off their new home!

TEAM LEADERS — 1979

Minutes Played: Birdsong, 2,839
Field-Goal Percentage: Robinzine, .548
Free-Throw Percentage: Ford, .813
Rebounds: Lacey, 702

Assists: Ford, 681
Steals: Ford, 174
Blocks: Lacey, 141
Scoring: Birdsong, 21.7

DRAFT CHOICES

1.	Reggie King	6-6	Alabama
2.	Choice to Los Angeles		
3.	Terry Crosby	6-4	Tennessee
4.	John McCullough	6-4	Oklahoma
5.	Curtis Watkins	6-5	DePaul
6.	Bob Roma	6-8	Princeton
7.	Nick Daniels	6-5	Xavier (OH)
8.	Tony Vann	6-6	Huntsville (AL)
9.	Gary Wilson	6-6	Southern Illinois
10.	Russell Saunders	6-0	New Mexico

DENVER NUGGETS

George McGinnis   Dan Issel

Every starter a superstar. That's the
pleasure — and the pain — of new coach
Donnie Walsh, who replaced Larry Brown
last February 1.

How can you argue with players like
David Thompson, George McGinnis,
Bobby Wilkerson, Charlie Scott, and Dan
Issel? Getting them to play together well
enough and often enough — that's
another story.

Thompson, the 6-4 jumping machine,
soars a mile high in the Mile High City. He
also tossed in 24.0 ppg in another All-Pro
season last year. 6-6 Charlie Scott, who
teams with Thompson at guard, seems to
have found a home in Denver after wan-
dering through the NBA for the previous
seven years. His 12.0 ppg and 428 assists
fit in nicely with Thompson's skywalking
game.

Away from his rivalry with Dr. J. in
Philadelphia, 6-8 George McGinnis had a

fine first year with the Nuggets. He led the team in rebounds (864) and steals (129), while scoring 22.6 ppg. Young (age 25) 6-7 Bobby Wilkerson (11.4), improving 6-5 Anthony Roberts (7.9), and question-mark 6-9 Bo Ellis (2.7) give Denver good depth at forward.

At age 31 and in his 10th pro year, Dan Issel (17.0) remains a potent force at center. The man they call "The Horse" lives up to his nickname through sheer hard work.

With no help from the draft, the Nuggets will do-or-die with practically the same cast as last year. Not a bad way to go!

TEAM LEADERS — 1979

Minutes Played: Issel, 2,742
Field-Goal Percentage: Boswell, .532
Free-Throw Percentage: Smith, .883
Rebounds: McGinnis, 864

Assists: Scott, 428
Steals: McGinnis, 129
Blocks: Hughes, 102
Scoring: Thompson, 24.0

DRAFT CHOICES

1.	Choice to Detroit		
2.	Gary Garland	6-4	DePaul
3.	Choice to Boston		
4.	Choice to Golden State		
5.	Larry Williams	6-8	Louisville
6.	Odell Ball	6-9	Marquette
7.	Nick Daniels	6-5	Xavier (OH)
8.	Matt Teahan	6-7	University of Denver
9.	Emmett Lewis	6-1	Colorado
10.	Choice to Chicago		

MILWAUKEE BUCKS

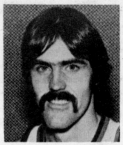

Quinn Buckner   **Brian Winters**

In Wisconsin, when Marques Johnson sneezes, everyone in the state calls the doctor. So when Marques said he was unhappy with his contract this pre-season, every Buck fan was unhappy. The 6-7, 218-pounder from UCLA is the spark plug in the Buck machine. The All-Pro pick threw in 25.6 ppg (third in the NBA) and led Milwaukee in 12 of 21 offensive departments.

So much for number one. The rest of the cast isn't bad, either. Hot-shot 6-4 Brian Winters (19.8) and steady 6-3 Quinn Buckner (7.2, 468 assists, and 156 steals) head the solid backcourt. For back-ups, there's super-quick 6-0 Lloyd Walton (5.0) and top draftee Sidney Moncrief of Arkansas.

Johnson is it at strong forward, but the rest of the front court could pose a problem. Big (6-11, 250) center Kent Benson (12.3) has never really made it as an NBA star. The Bucks hope that 6-9 Harvey

Catchings (obtained from New Jersey for John Gianelli) will push Benson to new heights.

Milwaukee's hopes at the second forward are keyed to the recovery of 6-8 Dave Meyers, who missed the '79 season. If Dave, known more in the pre-season as Ann Meyers' big brother, is healthy, 6-6 Ernie Grunfeld (10.3) and 6-5 Junior Bridgeman (15.5) will be excellent back-ups.

Buck fans also expect much from second draftee 6-10 Edgar Jones from Nevada-Reno. This is a good, young, exciting team — especially when Marques Johnson is happy.

TEAM LEADERS — 1979

Minutes Played: Johnson, 2,779
Field-Goal Percentage: Johnson, .550
Free-Throw Percentage: Winters, .856
Rebounds: Johnson, 586

Assists: Buckner, 468
Steals: Buckner, 156
Blocks: Johnson, 89
Scoring: Johnson, 25.6

DRAFT CHOICES

1.	Sidney Moncrief	6-4	Arkansas
2.	Edgar Jones	6-9	Nevada-Reno
3.	Larry Gibson	6-9½	Maryland
4.	Eugene Robinson	6-8	Northeastern Louisiana
5.	Jim Tillman	6-4	Eastern Kentucky
6.	Derrick Mayes	6-1	Illinois State
7.	Stan Ray	6-9	Cal. State Fullerton
8.	Larry Spicer	6-8	Alabama-Birmingham
9.	Roger Lapham	6-6	Maine
10.	Chris Fahrbach	6-7	North Dakota

CHICAGO BULLS

Artis Gilmore   **Ricky Sobers**

It took a couple of years, but Jerry Sloan is back as the Bulls' coach. Chicago fans can only hope that Jerry can do what Larry Costello and Scotty Robertson couldn't do last year: mold some good individual talent into a winning team. It's tougher than it sounds.

Though the Bulls were still playing "Let's Make a Deal" through the pre-season schedule, the problem was a basic one. Who would blend well with 6-7 All-Rookie guard Reggie Theus? Who could play up front with 7-1 Artis Gilmore? And so on.

Theus made a big splash as a big guard last season, with a 16.3 ppg average and a team-leading 429 assists. Gilmore led the team in almost every offensive and defensive department, including minutes played, shooting, rebounding, blocked shots, and scoring. His 23.7 ppg average was ninth best in the league.

If injury-prone (knees) Scott May is healthy, the Bulls could shape up quickly. The 6-7 ex-Indiana star played only 37 games last year and scored only 4.0 ppg.

Ex-Indiana Pacer Ricky Sobers (he replaced free-agent play-out Mickey Johnson) could tighten up the backcourt with Theus. Sobers nailed 17.3 ppg and made 138 steals for the '79 Pacers.

The free-agent market also brought 6-11 Coby Dietrick from San Antonio.

The draft produced UCLA's tough 6-9 Dave Greenwood and national college scoring champ 6-3 Lawrence Butler (30.1 ppg for Idaho State).

If the Bulls play as hard as their coach did, they'll be OK. Otherwise, it may be another long year in the Windy City.

TEAM LEADERS — 1979

Minutes Played: Gilmore, 3,265
Field-Goal Percentage: Gilmore, .575
Free-Throw Percentage:
  M. Johnson, .830
Rebounds: Gilmore, 1,043

Assists: Theus, 429
Steals: Holland, 122
Blocks: Gilmore, 156
Scoring: Gilmore, 23.7

DRAFT CHOICES

1.	Dave Greenwood	6-9	UCLA
2.	Lawrence Butler	6-3	Idaho State
3.	Calvin Garrett	6-7	Oral Roberts
3a.	Cedric Hordges	6-8	South Carolina
4.	George Maynor	6-3	East Carolina
5.	Larry Washington	6-0½	Drury (MO)
6.	Steve Smith	6-3	USC
7.	Mike Eversley	6-5	Chicago State
8.	Tony Warren	6-6	North Carolina State
9.	James Jackson	6-4	Minnesota
10.	Marvin Thomas	6-4	UCLA
10a.	Cortez Collins	6-6	Evansville

UTAH JAZZ

Bernard King

Adrian Dantley

The Louisiana judge who let the Jazz move to Utah may have been a real New Orleans fan. Maybe he couldn't bear to watch the home team anymore.

Under the New Orleans banner, the club had the worst record in the NBA last year. This time around, there are some new faces, a new coach, new scenery, and probably the same old result.

The Utah Jazz — the nickname makes about as much sense as the Sahara Lakers — start with tired, hobbling, 6-5 Pete Maravich. The not-so-hot Pistol did his best in '79, limping through 49 games and tossing in 22.6 points before taking the rest of the year off. But his 42.1% shooting was the pits. Will he bounce back in Utah? We'll see.

The new faces start with the coach — Tom Nissalke. The one-time boss of the ABA's Utah Stars is comfortable in Utah — but for how long? He's joined by the already well-traveled 6-5 Adrian Dantley. (The Lakers sent him in exchange for Spencer Haywood.) If Adrian, who averaged 17.3 ppg for L.A. last year, can ever put his act together, he could become a folk hero in Salt Lake City.

A pre-season trade with the Nets brought 6-7 small-forward Bernard King (21.6 ppg, 52.2% shooting), who has as much success on the court as he has trouble off it. Big (6-10) John Gianelli also came in the deal which cost Utah 7-0 Rich Kelley.

Other newcomers include 6-7 Allan Bristow (6.4) from San Antonio and 6-9 Ben Poquette (6.7) from Detroit, along with top draftee 6-8 Larry Knight of Chicago Loyola.

TEAM LEADERS — 1979

Minutes Played: McElroy, 2,698
Field-Goal Percentage: Kelley, .506
Free-Throw Percentage: Goodrich, .853
Rebounds: Kelley, 1,026

Assists: McElroy, 453
Steals: McElroy, 148
Blocks: Kelley, 166
Scoring: McElroy, 16.9*

*Truck Robinson averaged 24.2 ppg in 43 games with New Orleans; Pete Maravich averaged 22.6 ppg in 49 games; Spencer Haywood averaged 20.9 ppg for the season and 24.0 in his 34 games with the Jazz.

DRAFT CHOICES

1.	Choice to Los Angeles		
2.	Tico Brown	6-5	Georgia Tech
3.	Arvid Kramer	6-10	Augustana (SD)
4.	Greg Deane	6-6	Utah
5.	Perry Wolfe	6-2	Stanford
6.	Ernie Cobb	5-11	Boston College
7.	Paul Poe	6-8	Louisiana
8.	Keith McDonald	6-3	Utah State
9.	Milt Huggins	6-3	Southern Illinois
10.	Paul Dankins	6-2	Northern Illinois

WASHINGTON BULLETS

Kevin Grevey

Wes Unseld

NBA champs! NBA runners-up! Wouldn't you be happy with a two-year record of success like that? If you're running the Bullets you are — and you aren't.

Second place just wasn't good enough for Washington's Dick Motta and company. So they spent the off-season trying to improve the team.

Of course, any team that starts with a pair of All-Pros like 6-9 Elvin Hayes and 6-6 Bob Dandridge is on the right road in the first place. "Ironman" Hayes, who has missed only five games in his 11-year career, averaged 21.8 ppg and 12.1 rebounds last year. Super small-forward Dandridge wasn't far behind with a 20.4 ppg mark.

The biggest change? At point-guard, where the much-traveled 5-11 Kevin Porter (15.4 with Detroit) takes over from Tom

Henderson (now with Houston). NBA coaches say Porter, the league's assist leader (13.4 per game), is tough to control. But Bullet boss Dick Motta is sure he can do it.

With 6-3 Phil Chenier and 6-10 Mitch Kupchak question marks for 1980, Washington is looking at new blood. One new face, second-year man 6-6 Roger Phegley (2.8), was slated to be a starter when the team went to pre-season camp.

A healthy 6-5 Kevin Grevey (15.5) adds firepower to the Bullets' lineup, along with aging (but still tough) 6-7, 250-pound Wes Unseld (10.9 and 830 rebounds).

The draft (the Bullets had no first-round choice) provided little help.

TEAM LEADERS — 1979

Minutes Played: Hayes, 3,105
Field-Goal Percentage: Unseld, .577
Free-Throw Percentage: Dandridge, .825
Rebounds: Hayes, 994

Assists: Henderson, 419
Steals: Johnson, 95
Blocks: Hayes, 190
Scoring: Hayes, 21.8

DRAFT CHOICES

1.	Choice to Phoenix		
2.	Joe DeSantis	6-1	Fairfield
3.	Andrew Parker	6-5	Iowa State
3a.	Charles Floyd	6-7	High Point
4.	Lamont Reid	6-4	Oral Roberts
5.	Marshall Ashford	6-2	Virginia Tech
6.	Garcia Hopkins	6-6	Morgan State
7.	Picked Ineligible Player		
8.	Jo Jo Walters	6-4	Manhattan
9.	Ray Hooker	6-5½	Murray State
10.	Steve Martin	6-4	Georgetown

PHILADELPHIA 76ers

Doug Collins   **Darryl Dawkins**

If you can call a 47-35 season disappointing, then the Philly five was disappointing in 1979. If things don't get better in 1980, then coach Bill Cunningham could be in deep trouble.

The most crippling blow last year was a foot injury which sent 6-6 Doug Collins (19.5) from the court to the operating table on January 21. When Collins, star of the 1972 Olympic team, left the lineup, Cunningham had to scramble.

One positive result: the discovery of super-quick rookie 6-1 Maurice Cheeks (8.4). It also brought big men 6-11 Darryl Dawkins and 7-1 Caldwell Jones into the lineup together. Dawkins (13.1), who would only be a pro rookie this year if he hadn't skipped college, is slowly gaining control of his awesome game. Jones (9.3) was Philly's top rebounder and shotblocker.

Of course, the Doctor, 6-7 Julius Erving, is still one of the best. The three-time ABA scoring champ is just about the most exciting player in the NBA. Though his 1979 season wasn't one of his greatest (23.1 ppg, 7.2 rebounds, 357 assists, 35.9 minutes per game), it certainly wasn't bad.

Top rookie 6-5 Jim Spanarkel of Duke may beat out veteran 6-1 Henry Bibby for a spot in the Sixer backcourt. But with the years beginning to creep up on the Philly team, future drafts have to be more productive. After all, sub forward 6-8 Steve Mix (9.3 and the team's best shooter) is 32, Erving and Bibby are 30, Caldwell Jones is 29, etc. Even all-defensive star 6-9 Bobby Jones (12.1) is 28.

TEAM LEADERS — 1979

Minutes Played: Erving, 2,802
Field-Goal Percentage: Mix, .538
Free-Throw Percentage: Collins, .814
Rebounds: C. Jones, 747

Assists: Cheeks, 431
Steals: Cheeks, 174
Blocks: C. Jones, 157
Scoring: Erving, 23.1

DRAFT CHOICES

1.	Jim Spanarkel	6-5	Duke
2.	Clint Richardson	6-3	Seattle
2a.	Bernard Toone	6-8	Marquette
3.	Earl Cureton	6-9	Detroit
4.	Mike Niles	6-6	Cal. State Fullerton
5.	Carl McPipe	6-8	Nebraska
6.	Dan Hartshorne	6-10	Oregon
7.	Bobby Willis	6-2	Pennsylvania
8.	Rick Raivio	6-5	Portland
9.	Coby Leavitt	6-9	Utah
10.	Keith McCord	6-7	Alabama-Birmingham

NEW JERSEY NETS

Rich Kelley   **John Williamson**

Off a best-ever 37-45 season and a surprise playoff berth, the best pro basketball team in Piscataway, New Jersey, looks forward to an even better record in 1980 and its new Meadowlands arena in 1981.

The Nets, strong in the backcourt but thin up front, spent the off-season beefing up their forward line. Ex-Utah Jazz ace 7-0 Rich Kelley (12.8 rebounds pg) joins returning starter 6-11 George Johnson (the NBA's No. 2 shot-blocker at 3.24 per game) and 6-9 Bob Elliott, injured after only 14 games in '79.

Kelley, one of the six NBA players with more than 1,000 points (1253) and 1,000 rebounds (1026) a year ago, cost the Nets super small-forward Bernard King (21.6) and 6-10 John Gianelli. That opened up both forward spots on the club. 6-8 Jan van Breda Kolff had one of the spots most of last season, but his 6.7 ppg average makes his return there questionable.

However, Jan is one of the toughest defensive players in the league.

The backcourt is loaded, with 6-2 John Williamson (22.2) and 6-1 "Fast" Eddie Jordan (12.4, 365 assists, 201 steals — second in the NBA). Jordan's quick rise to stardom shocked even his greatest fans — and his original team, the Cleveland Cavaliers.

The Nets' draft seems super on paper, with 6-9 Cliff Robinson of USC and tough 6-5 Calvin "The Gnat" Natt of Northeastern Louisiana. The Nets, with their eye on that new 22,000-seat arena, hope both can make it big.

TEAM LEADERS — 1979

Minutes Played: King, 2,859
Field-Goal Percentage: King, .522
Free-Throw Percentage,
  Williamson, .854
Rebounds: King, 669

Assists: Jordan, 365
Steals: Jordan, 201
Blocks: Johnson, 253
Scoring: Williamson, 22.2

DRAFT CHOICES

1.	Calvin Natt	6-5	Northeastern Louisiana
1a.	Cliff Robinson	6-9	USC
2.	Choice to Detroit		
3.	John Gerdy	6-4	Davidson
4.	Choice to Seattle		
5.	Joe Abramaltis	6-8	Connecticut
6.	Tony Smith	6-1	Nevada-Las Vegas
7.	Jim Strickland	6-10	South Carolina
8.	Henry Hollingsworth	6-0	Hofstra
9.	Ricky Free	6-4	Columbia
10.	Eric Fleisher	6-1	Tulane

NEW YORK KNICKS

Marvin Webster   **Toby Knight**

While the Knicks got ready for the 1979-80 season on the court, the team's biggest problems were still in the courts. At stake: the 1978 payment for 7-1 Marvin Webster (11.3 and a team-high 655 rebounds in 60 games). The Knicks gave up big Lonnie Shelton, a first-draft choice, and a truckful of cash for the so-far disappointing Webster.

Marvin's newest problem — and the Knicks' latest "hope" — is 7-1 rookie Bill Cartwright. Bill averaged 24.5 points and 15.6 rebounds per game for the University of San Francisco last year. Webster's knee problems made Cartwright's arrival even more important.

The New Yorkers' top returning scorer, 6-2 Ray Williams (17.3), has all the tools — but makes too many mistakes. His backcourt mates have problems, too. 6-4 Jim Cleamons (9.5) doesn't score enough. 6-3½ Earl Monroe (12.3) is too old (35).

Perhaps the outstanding Knick last year was 6-9 Toby Knight. Now in his third year, Knight comes off a 16.6 ppg, 548 rebound season. His main off-season gripe: money — not enough coming his way.

As the season opened, the Knicks were still making changes. If the team's won-lost record (31-51 last year, 23 games behind division leader Washington) doesn't change quickly, the next change might involve coach Red Holzman.

TEAM LEADERS — 1979

Minutes Played: Knight, 2,667
Field-Goal Percentage: Knight, .519
Free-Throw Percentage: Monroe, .838
Rebounds: Webster, 655

Assists: Williams, 504
Steals: Williams, 128
Blocks: Webster, 112
Scoring: Williams, 17.3*

*Bob McAdoo averaged 26.9 ppg in 40 games with the Knicks; Spencer Haywood averaged 17.8 ppg in 34 games.

DRAFT CHOICES

1.	Bill Cartwright	7-1	San Francisco
1a.	Larry Demic	6-9	Arizona
1b.	"Sly" Williams	6-7	Rhode Island
2.	Reggie Carter	6-3	St. John's (NY)
2a.	Kim Goetz	6-7	San Diego State
3.	Geoff Huston	6-1	Texas Tech
4.	Larry Rogers	6-6	Southeastern Missouri State
5.	Johnny Green	6-7	Cal.-Riverside
6.	Phil Abney	6-5	New Mexico
7.	Marc Coleman	6-5	Seton Hall
8.	Billy Tucker	6-5	Tennessee State
9.	Brett Wyatt	6-3	Jersey City State
10.	Gordon Thomas	6-3	St. John's (NY)

BOSTON CELTICS

Chris Ford

Earl Tatum

Last time coach Bill Fitch started a new job, he skippered the expansion (spelled A-W-F-U-L) Cleveland Cavaliers. That's why things have to look good to him in Boston, even though he's taking over a last-place (29-53) ball club.

The good news: There's hard-working 6-6 M. L. Carr. The ex-Detroit Piston averaged 18.7 ppg and a league-leading 2.46 steals per game last season. He came to Boston as a free agent (the compensation was former All-Pro Bob McAdoo) over the summer.

Carr joins long-awaited 6-10 rookie Larry Bird, star of Indiana State's national runners-up, 6-9 former Celtic coach Dave Cowens (16.6 in 68 games), and NBA shooting leader 6-8 Cornbread Maxwell to form one of the toughest front lines in the league.

The backcourt is Fitch's trouble area. There's no shortage of experience. Boston's guards include 11-year-man 6-5 Don Chaney (5.9), nine-year-man 6-1 Tiny Archibald (11.0), five-year-man 6-5 Kevin Stacom (4.4), and seven-year-man 6-5 Chris Ford (15.4). But that's not a backcourt of which championships are made. 6-6 Jeff Judkins, a late-closer as a rookie last year (8.8), provides some depth at guard.

The Celts got no help in the draft. McAdoo cost them three first-round draft choices. But Fitch thinks he has a decent shot at the playoffs his first time around.

TEAM LEADERS — 1979

Minutes Played: Maxwell, 2,969
Field-Goal Percentage: Maxwell, .584
Free-Throw Percentage: Cowens, .807
Rebounds: Maxwell, 791

Assists: Ford, 374
Steals: Ford, 115
Blocks: Maxwell, 74
Scoring: Maxwell, 19.0*

*Bob McAdoo averaged 24.8 ppg for the season and 20.6 ppg in his 20 games with the Celtics.

DRAFT CHOICES

1.	Choice to New York		
2.	Choice to Phoenix		
3.	Wayne Kreklow	6-4	Drake
3a.	Ernesto Malcolm	6-4	Briarcliff
4.	Nick Galis	6-1	Seton Hall
5.	Jimmy Allen	6-3	New Haven
6.	Marvin Delph	6-4	Arkansas
7.	Steve Castellan	6-8	Virginia
8.	Glenn Sudhop	7-0	North Carolina State
9.	Kevin Sinnett	6-6	Navy
10.	Alton Byrd	5-8	Columbia

SAN ANTONIO SPURS

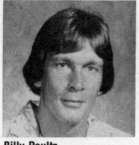

Billy Paultz   **Larry Kenon**

The Spurs — and coach Doug Moe — may be in trouble. In the improving Central Division, the Spurs may not be improving enough.

You can't argue with their backcourt. 6-7 George Gervin is basketball's No. 1 point machine, the first guard in pro history to ever lead the league in scoring twice in a row. Can he average 29.6 ppg again? Why not?

His running mate, 6-3 James Silas, has bounced back from two years of knee problems to re-establish himself as a top pro guard. (He was one of the ABA's all-time best.) His 16.0 ppg average is only part of the story. He's a complete player. Veteran 6-4 Mike Gale (8.0) led the Spurs in assists (374), and is a fine back-up.

The question marks are up front. 6-9 Larry Kenon (22.1), the team's rebounding and steals leader, spent the off-season unhappy (over money, what else?). "The Whopper," 6-11, 250-pound center Billy Paultz (11.5), is coming off an off-year. 6-9 Mark Olberding (9.4) rounds out the tremendous front line, with back-up help from 6-10 Mike Green (7.5).

Gone are 6-7 Allan Bristow (free agent to Utah for 6-9 Paul Griffin), 6-11 Coby Dietrick (free agent to Chicago), and 6-0 three-point-goal shooting guard Louie Dampier (to New Jersey). The top draftee, 6-7 Wiley Peck of Mississippi State, may help up front — especially if he plays defense. It's one subject that the high-scoring Spurs don't seem to know much about.

TEAM LEADERS — 1979

Minutes Played: Kenon, 2,947
Field-Goal Percentage: Gervin, .541
Free-Throw Percentage: Kenon, .845
Rebounds: Kenon, 790

Assists: Gale, 374
Steals: Kenon, 154
Blocks: Paultz, 125
Scoring: Gervin, 29.6

DRAFT CHOICES

1.	Wiley Peck	6-7	Mississippi State
2.	Choice to Portland		
3.	Sylvester Norris	6-11	Jackson State
4.	Al Daniel	6-4	Furman
5.	Steve Schall	6-11	Arkansas
6.	Terry Knight	6-5	Pittsburgh
7.	Tyrone Branyan	6-7	Texas
8.	Selected Ineligible Player		
9.	Eddie McLeod	6-8	Nevada-Las Vegas
10.	Glen Fine	5-10	Harvard

HOUSTON ROCKETS

Rudy Tomjanovich   Calvin Murphy

New coach Del Harris isn't in a bad spot. The silver-haired, 41-year-old starts his career as a pro boss with a 47-35 club and the league MVP (Moses Malone).

The 6-10, 235-pound Malone finally put his act all together in his fifth pro season. His dominance of the backboards, especially at the offensive end, tells you that the man has an unlimited future. He also threw in 24.8 ppg in '79.

But Moses didn't lead the Rockets closer to the Promised Land all by himself. ("If it wasn't for my teammates and all their missed shots," he said, "I could never have grabbed as many offensive bounds.") There's well-traveled 6-8 Rick Barry (13.5). At 35 he's lost half a step or so. But his free-throw shooting (94.7%, a league record) was never better.

There's 5-10 (or less) Cal Murphy (20.2), the league's second-best foul shooter (92.8%), and the Rockets' floor leader.

70

There's 6-8 Rudy T. (for Tomjanovich), who bounced back from his memorable fight with Kermit Washington to average 19.0 ppg and pluck down 572 rebounds. And there's 6-3 former Bullet Tom Henderson (10.8), who came to Houston during the summer as a free agent. Coach Harris hopes he'll do the job as the team's point-guard.

The bench, with 6-8 third-year-man Robert Reid (10.9) and gritty 6-5 Mike Newlin (10.2), needs more help. Since Harris has a one-year contract, he'll work hard to find it.

TEAM LEADERS — 1979

Minutes Played: Malone, 3,390
Field-Goal Percentage: Malone, .540
Free-Throw Percentage: Barry, .947
Rebounds: Malone, 1,444

Assists: Barry, 502
Steals: Murphy, 117
Blocks: Malone, 119
Scoring: Malone, 24.8

DRAFT CHOICES

1.	Lee Johnson	6-11	East Texas State
2.	Paul Mokeski	7-0	Kansas
3.	Ricardo Brown	6-0	Pepperdine
4.	Lionel Green	6-4	LSU
5.	Allen Leavell	6-1	Oklahoma City
6.	Collie Davis	6-5	Southern (LA)
7.	Rich Valavicius	6-5	Auburn
8.	Delbert Watson	6-2	Eastern Tennessee State
9.	PASS		
10.	PASS		

ATLANTA HAWKS

John Drew **Armond Hill**

It's still hard to believe that the Hawks are for real. Without super personnel, the club has gone from a 31-51 mark in 1977 to 41-41 in '78 and 46-36 in '79. That's one reason why any discussion of Coach-of-the-Year honors begins with Hawk boss Hubie Brown.

Under Brown, the Hawks play a team offense and hard-nosed defense. There's good strength up front with 6-8 Dan Roundfield, who came to Atlanta as a free agent from Indiana. In his first Georgia winter, Dan averaged 15.3 ppg, along with 10.8 rebounds (10th in the league) and 2.2 blocks (seventh in the league). 6-6 John Drew, last of the pre-Brown Hawks, had another outstanding year, scoring 22.7 ppg (12th best in the NBA) to lead Atlanta for the fifth straight year. 6-9 Steve Hawes (10.5) is adequate at center.

Young 6-4 Terry Furlow, who came to Atlanta from Cleveland (for Butch Lee) early last season, was a pleasant surprise (12.0). The NBA's new three-point field-goal rule should benefit Furlow, but Atlanta's starting guards should still be 6-2 Eddie Johnson (16.0), the Hawks' No. 2 scorer in '79, and 6-4 Armond Hill, one of the smartest players in the business.

For depth, the Hawks have such as mighty mite 5-7 Charlie Criss (5.3), and the slightly taller 7-1 Tree Rollins (8.4), the team's leading shot-blocker in '79.

TEAM LEADERS — 1979

Minutes Played: Roundfield, 2,539
Field-Goal Percentage: Johnson, .510*
Free-Throw Percentage: Hill, .854
Rebounds: Roundfield, 865

Assists: Hill, 480
Steals: Drew, 128
Blocks: Rollins, 254
Scoring: Drew, 22.7

*Rollins hit .535 from the field, but failed to qualify.

DRAFT CHOICES

1.	Choice to Indiana		
2.	James Bradley	6-8	Memphis State
2a.	Larry Wilson	6-6	Nicholls State
3.	Don Marsh	6-0	Franklin & Marshall
4.	Choice to Los Angeles		
5.	Tiny Pinder	6-7	North Carolina State
6.	Dwight Williams	6-0	Gardner-Webb
7.	Tim Waterman	6-8½	St. Bonaventure
8.	John Goedeke	6-9	Maryland-Baltimore Co.
9.	Cedric Oliver	6-4	Hamilton (NY)
10.	Chad Nelson	6-10	Drake

Central Division
CLEVELAND CAVALIERS

Campy Russell

Jim Chones

The folks who run the Cavaliers seem to know what they're doing. Before hiring Stan Albeck as their new head coach last summer, they had several meetings with the players. That should make the squad very happy. Now, if they'll play for the man, it should make the owners very happy.

Unfortunately, Albeck doesn't have much more to work with than the last coach, Bill Fitch (now with Boston). 6-8 forward Campy Russell (21.9) can hit from anywhere and was the Cavs' top assist man, too. 5-11 Footsie Walker (10.1) can dazzle opponents with his quick hands and, of course, feet. His 2.36 steals per game was fourth best in the league.

Jim Chones (13.4), a one-time ABA bust, is turning into a solid rebounder (842) and defender. But the 6-11 Chones must score more. 7-0 Elmore Smith (6.5) teams nicely with Chones — when he's healthy. Smith missed 58 games last year.

Former San Diego Clipper speed-burner 6-3 Randy Smith is the newest Cav. He came over in the post-Walton compensation days for a top draft choice. Randy's 20.5 scoring last year was second only to "All-World" Free among the Clippers. If 6-4 Walt Frazier, who played only 12 games last season, returns to form, the already strong Cleveland backcourt will be stronger.

With little apparent help in the draft, Albeck's road to a title won't be easy, no matter who picked him for the job.

TEAM LEADERS — 1979

Minutes Played: Russell, 2,859
Field-Goal Percentage: Mitchell, .513
Free-Throw Percentage: Carr, .816
Rebounds: Chones, 842

Assists: Russell, 348
Steals: Walker, 130
Blocks: Chones, 102
Scoring: Russell, 21.9

DRAFT CHOICES

1.	Choice to Detroit		
2.	Bruce Flowers	6-8	Notre Dame
3.	Bill Laimbeer	6-10	Notre Dame
4.	Rick Swing	6-3	Citadel
5.	Matt Simpkins	6-5	Georgia Southern
6.	Jon Manning	6-2	North Texas State
7.	Steve Skaggs	6-5	Ohio University
8.	Mark Haymore	6-8	Massachusetts
9.	Tim Joyce	6-5	Ohio University
10.	Terry Peavy	6-4	Point Park (PA)

DETROIT PISTONS

Bob Lanier   **Bob McAdoo**

Hard-working coach Dick Vitale has his work cut out trying to turn around last season's 30-52 Pistons.

Putting the ball in the basket should be a snap. A healthy(?) 6-11 Bob Lanier is able to score anytime. He tallied 23.6 per outing last year, but missed 29 games with a knee problem that doesn't seem to go away.

Last year's most dependable player, 6-6 M. L. Carr (18.7, 197 steals), is now a Boston Celtic (as a free-agent signee). The deal made 6-10 scoring-machine Bob McAdoo a Piston. The ex-North Carolina ace tossed in 24.8 ppg for Boston and the Knicks in '79. But what he doesn't know about defense could fill several books the size of this one.

There's good young talent with 6-7 All-Rookie choice Terry Tyler (12.9), 6-5 John Long (16.1 as a freshman), and 6-3 ex-Jazz guard James McElroy (16.9 ppg, 453 assists, and 148 steals). Detroit hopes McElroy will replace little Kevin Porter (15.4), the league-leading assist man (1,099). He played out his option and signed with Eastern champ Washington.

The key to Detroit's 1980 fortunes is in the hands of the rookies. Coach Vitale was pleased with the fresh crop which brought him 6-7 Greg Kelser, co-star of Michigan State's national college champs, UCLA's 6-2 Roy Hamilton, and Michigan's 6-8 Phil Hubbard, a college All-American as a sophomore and an injury victim thereafter.

Detroit is a team with potential — but maybe not this season!

TEAM LEADERS — 1979

Minutes Played: Carr, 3,207
Field-Goal Percentage: Lanier, .515
Free-Throw Percentage: Long, .826
Rebounds: Douglas, 664

Assists: Porter, 1,099
Steals: Carr, 197
Blocks: Douglas, 201
Scoring: Carr, 18.7*

*Bob Lanier averaged 23.6 ppg, but played in only 53 games and scored only 1,253 points. NBA requires 70 games or 1,400 points to qualify.

DRAFT CHOICES

1.	Greg Kelser	6-7	Michigan State
1a.	Roy Hamilton	6-2	UCLA
1b.	Phil Hubbard	6-7	Michigan
2.	Tony Price	6-7	Pennsylvania
3.	Terry Duerod	6-2	Detroit
4.	Choice to Milwaukee		
5.	Flintie Williams	6-3	Nevada-Las Vegas
6.	Truman Claytor	6-1	Kentucky
7.	Ken Jones	6-1	St. Mary's (CA)
8.	Rodney Lee	6-6	Memphis State
9.	Val Bracey	6-2	Central Michigan
10.	Willie Polk	6-5	Grand Canyon (AZ)

INDIANA PACERS

James Edwards   **Johnny Davis**

The Pacers have a new address. No, they're still playing their home games at Indianapolis's Market Square Arena. But you'll find their record under the NBA's Central Division umbrella. That could improve the team's 1980 playoff hopes.

Actually, the Pacers' 38-44 record a year ago would have been good enough for the final Eastern playoff berth. Indiana won 12 of its last 17 and 22 of its last 36 in '79. Can they keep it up?

There's plenty of firepower in the backcourt with 6-2 Johnny David (18.3), the team's leading scorer, and 6-6 Billy Knight (14.3), picked up from Boston at mid-season. (5-9 Ann Meyers of UCLA was an early training-camp dropout.)

Up front, 7-1 James Edwards (16.7) and 6-9 Len Elmore (4.2) provide strength at center. Edwards is coming fast, though Elmore has been somewhat of a disappointment over his five NBA seasons.

Ex-Chicago Bull 6-10 Mickey Johnson (15.4) joins 6-9 Mike Bantom (14.7) and 6-7 Alex English (16.0). Though Johnson cost Indiana the services of backcourt star Ricky Sobers, his addition gives the team a powerful forward trio.

Coach Bob Leonard hopes that top draft pick 6-6 guard-forward Dudley Bradley of North Carolina follows his college teammates Walt Davis and Phil Ford as NBA Rookie of the Year. 6-8 Tony Zeno of Arizona State could fit in at forward.

TEAM LEADERS — 1979

Minutes Played: J. Davis, 2,971
Field-Goal Percentage: Knight, .528
Free-Throw Percentage: Sobers, .882
Rebounds: Edwards, 693

Assists: J. Davis, 453
Steals: Sobers, 138
Blocks: Edwards, 109
Scoring: J. Davis, 18.3

DRAFT CHOICES

1.	Dudley Bradley	6-6	North Carolina
2.	Tony Zeno	6-8	Arizona State
3.	Choice to Boston		
4.	Don Newman	6-3	Idaho
5.	Billy Reid	6-4	San Francisco
6.	Greg Guye	6-7	Stetson
7.	Dirk Ewing	6-4	Stetson
8.	Brian Magid	6-2	George Washington
9.	PASS		
10.	PASS		

1978-79
N.B.A. STANDINGS

EASTERN CONFERENCE

Atlantic Division

	W	L	Pct.	GB
Washington	54	28	.659	--
Philadelphia	47	35	.573	7
New Jersey	37	45	.451	17
New York	31	51	.378	23
Boston	29	53	.354	25

Central Division

	W	L	Pct.	GB
San Antonio	48	34	.585	--
Houston	47	35	.573	1
Atlanta	46	36	.561	2
Cleveland	30	52	.366	18
Detroit	30	52	.366	18
New Orleans	26	56	.317	22

WESTERN CONFERENCE

Midwest Division

	W	L	Pct.	GB
Kansas City	48	34	.585	--
Denver	47	35	.573	1
Indiana	38	44	.463	10
Milwaukee	38	44	.463	10
Chicago	31	51	.378	17

Pacific Division

	W	L	Pct.	GB
Seattle	52	30	.634	--
Phoenix	50	32	.610	2
Los Angeles	47	35	.573	5
Portland	45	35	.549	7
San Diego	43	39	.524	9
Golden St.	38	44	.463	14

1978-79 STATISTICS

George Gervin

INDIVIDUAL SCORING

Minimum 70 games played or 1,400 points

	G	FG	FT	PTS.	AVG.
Gervin, S.A.	80	947	471	2365	29.6
Free, S.D.	78	795	654	2244	28.8
M. Johnson, Mil.	77	820	332	1972	25.6
McAdoo, Bos.	60	596	295	1487	24.8
Malone, Hou.	82	716	599	2031	24.8
Thompson, Den.	76	693	439	1825	24.0
Westphal, Phoe.	81	801	339	1941	24.0
Abdul-Jabbar, L.A.	80	777	349	1903	23.8
Gilmore, Chi.	82	753	434	1940	23.7
Davis, Phoe.	79	764	340	1868	23.6
Erving, Phil.	78	715	373	1803	23.1
Drew, Atl.	79	650	495	1795	22.7
McGinnis, Den.	76	603	509	1715	22.6
Williamson, N.J.	74	635	373	1643	22.2
Kenon, S.A.	81	748	295	1791	22.1
Russell, Clev.	74	603	417	1623	21.9
Hayes, Wash.	82	720	349	1789	21.8
Birdsong, K.C.	82	741	296	1778	21.7
King, N.J.	82	710	349	1769	21.6
Robinson, Phoe.	69	566	324	1456	21.1

FIELD GOALS

Minimum 300 Made

	FG	FGA	PCT.
Maxwell, Bos.	472	808	.584
Abdul-Jabbar, L.A.	777	1347	.577
Unseld, Wash.	346	600	.577
Gilmore, Chi.	753	1310	.575
Nater, S.D.	357	627	.569
Washington, S.D.	350	623	.562
Davis, Phoe.	764	1362	.561
M. Johnson, Mil.	820	1491	.550
Robinzine, K.C.	459	837	.548
Owens, Port.	600	1095	.548

Cedric Maxwell

FREE THROWS

Minimum 125 Made

	FT	FTA	PCT.
Barry, Hou.	160	169	.947
Murphy, Hou.	246	265	.928
Brown, Sea.	183	206	.888
Smith, Den.	159	180	.883
Sobers, Ind.	298	338	.882
White, G.S.	139	158	.880
Twardzik, Port.	261	299	.873
Newlin, Hou.	212	243	.872
Dunleavy, Hou.	159	184	.864
Winters, Mil.	237	277	.856

Rick Barry

Kevin Porter

ASSISTS

Minimum 70 games or 400 assists

	G	NO.	AVG.
Porter, Det.	82	1099	13.4
Lucas, G.S.	82	762	9.3
Nixon, L.A.	82	737	9.0
Ford, K.C.	79	681	8.6
Westphal, Phoe.	81	529	6.5
Barry, Hou.	80	502	6.3
Williams, N.Y.	81	504	6.2
Henderson, Wash.	70	419	6.0
Hill, Atl.	82	480	5.9
Buckner, Mil.	81	468	5.8

Kareem Abdul-Jabbar

BLOCKED SHOTS

Minimum 70 games or 100 blocked shots

	G	NO.	AVG.
Abdul-Jabbar, L.A.	80	316	3.95
Johnson, N.J.	78	253	3.24
Rollins, Atl.	81	254	3.14
Parish, G.S.	76	217	2.86
Tyler, Det.	82	201	2.45
Hayes, Wash.	82	190	2.32
Roundfield, Atl.	80	176	2.20
Kelley, N.O.	80	166	2.08
C. Jones, Phil.	78	157	2.01
Gilmore, Chi.	82	156	1.90

STEALS

Minimum 70 games or 125 steals

	G	NO.	AVG.
Carr, Det.	80	197	2.46
Jordan, N.J.	82	201	2.45
Nixon, L.A.	82	201	2.45
Walker, Clev.	55	130	2.36
Ford, K.C.	79	174	2.20
Smith, S.D.	82	177	2.16
Cheeks, Phil.	82	174	2.12
Williams, Sea.	76	158	2.08
Porter, Det.	82	158	1.93
Buckner, Mil.	81	156	1.93

M.L. Carr

REBOUNDS

Minimum 70 games or 800 rebounds

	G	OFF	DEF	TOT	AVG.
Malone, Hou.	82	587	857	1444	17.6
Kelley, N.O.	80	303	723	1026	12.8
Abdul-Jabbar, L.A.	80	207	818	1025	12.8
Gilmore, Chi.	82	293	750	1043	12.7
Sikma, Sea.	82	232	781	1013	12.4
Hayes, Wash.	82	312	682	994	12.1
Parish, G.S.	76	265	651	916	12.1
Robinson, Phoe.	69	195	607	802	11.6
McGinnis, Den.	76	256	608	864	11.4
Roundfield, Atl.	80	326	539	865	10.8

Moses Malone

OPENING GAME ROSTERS

Atlantic Division

Bullets: Porter, *Malovic* (injured), Dandridge, Hayes, Bailey, Phegley, Kupchak (injured), Wright, Grevey, Corzine, Unseld, Ballard, Chenier.

76ers: Erving, Cheeks, C. Jones, Bibby, Collins, Money, B. Jones, Skinner (injured), *Toone*, *Spanarkel*, *Richardson* (injured), Mix, Dawkins.

Nets: Newlin, Jordan, van Breda Kolff, Bassett, Williamson, Boynes, *Natt*, Simpson, *Robinson*, Johnson, Kelley, Elliott (injured).

Knicks: R. Williams, Monroe (injured), Richardson, *Huston*, *Cartwright*, *S. Williams*, Glenn, Cleamons, Webster (injured), *Demic*, Knight, *Copeland*, Meriweather.

Celtics: Archibald, Chaney, Cowens, Carr, Maxwell, Judkins, *Bird*, Ford, *Henderson*, Fernsten, Robey.

Central Division:

Spurs: *Evans*, Paultz, Gale, Silas, *Kiffin*, Griffin, Restani, Kenon, *Norris* (injured), Gervin, Olberding, *Peck*.

Rockets: Barry, Henderson, Dunleavy, *M. Jones*, D. Jones, Bradley, Murphy, Malone, *Leavell* (injured), White, Dorsey (injured), Tomjanovich, Reid, *Mokeski* (injured).

Hawks: Johnson, Hawes, Criss, Givens, Drew, Hill, Furlow, Rollings, Roundfield, Lee, McMillen, *Wilson* (injured).

Cavaliers: E. Smith (injured), B. Smith, R. Smith, Frazier, W. Smith, Walker (injured), Lee (injured), Russell, Lambert, Robisch, Mitchell, Willoughby, Carr, Tatum.

Pistons: McAdoo, Douglas, Lanier, *Evans* (injured), *Hamilton*, Long, *Kelser*, McElroy, Shumate, *Hubbard*, Tyler, *Duerod*.

Pacers: Kuester (injured), M. Johnson, Calhoun,

Bradley, J. Davis, English, Knight, B. Davis, Edwards, Elmore (injured), Bantom, *Zeno*, C. Johnson.

Midwest Division

Kings: Ford, Redmond, Birdsong, Wedman, Burleson (injured), Grunfeld, Gerard, Green, McKinney, Lacey, *King*, Robinzine.

Nuggets: Roche, Scott, Roberts, *Garland*, McGinnis, Ellis, Wilkerson, Thompson, Hughes, Boswell, Issel.

Bucks: Bridgeman, *Moncrief*, *Cummings*, Meyers, M. Johnson, Walton, Buckner, G. Johnson (injured), Washington, Winters, Catchings, Benson.

Bulls: Beshore, Mengelt, May, Theus, Dietrick, Johnson, *Greenwood*, Sobers, Gilmore, Landsberger, Brown.

Jazz: Dantley, Smith, Maravich, Hardy, *Williams*, King, *Dawkins*, *Deane*, Gianelli, Bristow, Poquette, *Kilpatrick* (injured).

Pacific Division

SuperSonics: Williams, Shelton, *V. Johnson*, *Bailey*, LaGarde, D. Johnson, J. Johnson, Brown, Silas, Walker, Sikma.

Suns: Davis, Buse, *High*, Scott, Robinson, Bratz, Heard, Adams, Forrest (injured), Westphal, *Cook*, Kramer.

Lakers: Carr, Chones, Nixon, *White* (injured), *Holland*, Cooper, Boone, *Mack* (injured), Haywood, Johnson, Abdul-Jabbar, Ford, Wilkes.

Trail Blazers: *Paxson*, Hollins, Brewer, *Jeelani*, Twardzik (injured), Steele, Lucas (injured), Dunn, Owens, Gross, Washington, Thompson (injured), Kunnert, Brewer.

Clippers: Weatherspoon, Taylor, Williams, Wicks, Pietkiewicz, Bryant, Free, Carrington, Nater, Walton, Whitehead, Olive (injured), Lee (injured).

Warriors: Parish, Lucas, Abernethy, White, Townsend, *Wilson*, Smith (injured), Parker, *Coughran*, Cooper, Ray, Short.

Note: Rookies in *italics*.